Contents

What are habitats?

Habitats are places where wildlife lives. Some habitats, such as rivers or the seashore, have formed naturally and are very big. Others, such as hedgerows or gardens, are smaller and are made by people.

Rivers are **natural** habitats. They are home to many plants and animals, such as this water vole.

The seashore is home to seaweed, gulls, crabs and sea anemones like the one below.

Many different animals live in a hedgerow. Most hedgerows are planted by farmers.

Looking at habitats

You won't find crabs in a forest or bluebells in the sea. That's because animals and plants can only live in a habitat that suits them. The wildlife that lives in a particular habitat may find it hard living anywhere else.

Squirrel ▲

◄ Deer

Forests are shady places full of trees. They suit many different animals and plants.

Bluebell ▶

◀ Dragonfly

Some wildlife prefers a
damp habitat, such as
a river or pond.

Frog ▶

Living together

The animals and plants that live in a habitat depend on one another. Big animals feed on smaller animals, and the smallest animals often feed on plants. Each **species** is an important link in the **food chain**.

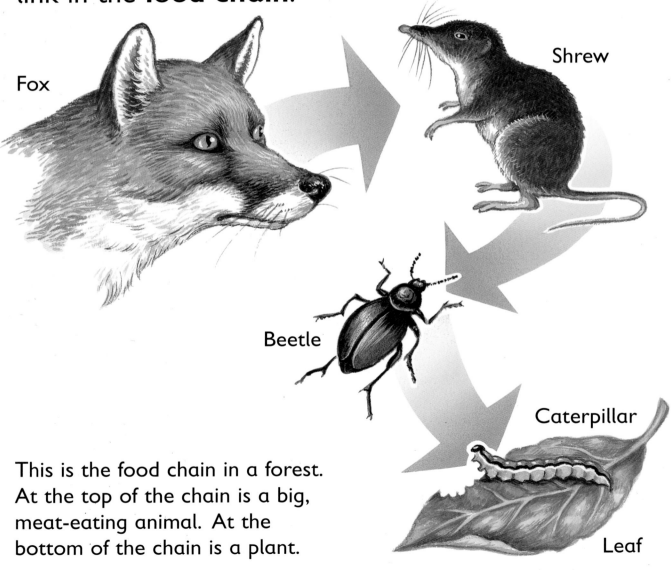

Fox

Shrew

Beetle

Caterpillar

Leaf

This is the food chain in a forest. At the top of the chain is a big, meat-eating animal. At the bottom of the chain is a plant.

Bees feed on the nectar in the flowers that grow in gardens and parks.

Animals depend on the plants in their habitat. A swan hides her young among the reeds that grow at the water's edge.

Damage to habitats

Most habitats take a long time to form but they can be damaged very quickly. This happens when they are **polluted** or used for building or farming.

This used to be a habitat of trees and fields. Now roads and railways have been built in their place.

▲ Many kinds of plants grew in this meadow. Now the land has been used for building and the plants have disappeared.

Foxes, hedgehogs and other animals hunt in these hedges. Where will they find food if all of the hedges are destroyed? ▼

Litter

People often drop litter in wildlife habitats. Litter is ugly. It pollutes the **environment**, and can be dangerous to animals. Look carefully at this picture and try to spot some of the problems.

There is a shopping trolley in the river. It is a danger to waterbirds and other creatures.

Broken glass bottles have sharp edges. They can cut animals badly.

Empty cans are traps for small animals. They crawl inside, but can't get out.

This bird has put its head inside a plastic ring. In time, the ring could kill the bird.

Plastic bags have been thrown in the water. Animals try and feed on them and may be poisoned.

Someone is throwing paint into the river. This will pollute the water and kill fish and tiny creatures.

Litter is dirty and makes a place look so bad that people no longer care about it.

A better way with litter

There are ways of getting rid of litter. You can see some ideas in the picture below. Litter-free places make better habitats and they look much nicer, too.

There are rubbish bins for people to use.

These children are collecting litter and putting it in the bin.

The river banks are a clean, safe habitat for animals and plants.

The water is much cleaner. There are more fish and other creatures living in it now.

The hedges and bushes along the river bank make safe habitats for small animals and birds.

The place looks much nicer. People are enjoying and using it more, and they will want to protect it.

Polluting the soil

Most of the farmers who grow our food use all sorts of powders and sprays. These kill **pests** and help crops to grow, but they also pollute the soil and harm wildlife. **Organic** farming is kinder to the environment.

Powerful sprays kill pests but they can also poison butterflies and other harmless creatures.

▲ Farmers use **fertilizers** to grow better crops. Rain washes fertilizers into streams, where they pollute the water.

Organic food is grown using ▶ natural fertilizers. Organic farming protects wildlife and does not pollute the environment.

Life-giving plants

Plants are very important. They provide all sorts of wonderful foods and help to build the structure of the soil. Most importantly, plants produce a **gas** called **oxygen**. Humans and other animals breathe oxygen. Without it, we could not survive.

Plants provide all kinds of food. We feed on their flowers, fruits, leaves and roots.

▲ We need to plant more trees. The air in our cities is often polluted. Trees help to keep it clean.

Trees and ▶ other plants make oxygen in their leaves. A large forest produces a huge amount of oxygen.

Protecting animals

When people spoil or destroy habitats, the animals that live in them slowly disappear. Animals need our protection. We need to look after their habitats, and make new ones wherever we can.

Some animals, such as this dormouse, can only live in one kind of habitat. If their habitat is polluted or destroyed, they may become **endangered** or **extinct**.

Cleaning polluted habitats helps to protect wildlife. Otters cannot live in polluted rivers but they return when rivers are cleaned.

Wildlife in our towns

Our towns are changing. With more people, more houses, and more roads, habitats are disappearing. What happens to the wildlife in these places? What happens to our towns? Look carefully at the picture to see some of the problems.

Many gardens are paved over to make a parking space for cars.

The streets are full of cars and trucks. The air is dirty with **fumes**.

There are no green spaces for people to enjoy.

There are no
trees in the
streets.

There is nothing but brick and
concrete. There are no plants to
provide homes or food for wildlife.

23

A better way for wildlife

Every town and city has room for plants.
Plants provide animals with shelter and food.
They also improve the environment.
Can you see what has happened in
the picture below?

A pond makes a habitat for dragonflies and other creatures.

Trees have been planted along the streets. Their leaves help to clean the air.

A pile of damp logs is home to snails, beetles and many creepy-crawlies.

Worms burrow among the leaves under a hedge. They are food for the birds.

Window-boxes and tubs make homes for insects.

Someone has sown wildflower seeds. Insects now feed on the flowers.

Bird tables help birds to survive the winter. Berry bushes provide food, too.

Small actions, big results

Is it possible for you to protect habitats? Of course, it is! And if your small steps are copied by millions of other people, the results for wildlife will be huge! Everyone on Earth shares the planet. Everyone can help to save it.

What would happen if people didn't pollute the environment?

With no pollution, our land, air, rivers and seas would be clean and safe. This would improve the world around us and make better habitats for animals and plants.

> *What would happen if everyone planted trees?*

More trees would help to clean the air and provide plenty of oxygen. Trees are beautiful and make wonderful habitats. They supply wildlife with shelter and food.

> *What would happen if everyone protected animal habitats?*

If everyone protected habitats there would be a much richer mix of animals and plants, and their numbers would grow. We would all enjoy living in a world full of wildlife.

Over to you!

No one wants wildlife to disappear. Why not try one of the ideas below, and help to protect habitats?

Design posters to encourage people to pick up litter and improve the environment. Stick them up at home, at school, in your library or club house.

If you have a garden, find out which trees and bushes are best for wildlife. Ask your parents to plant them.

If you don't have a garden, plant a tub or windowbox. You will have many insect visitors.

Grow your own organic foods either in a growbag or the garden. Rot down old fruit and vegetable peelings to make a **compost** for your plants.

Try and persuade your parents to buy organic food.

In the autumn, collect seeds from trees and plant them in pots. The following year, try and find places where the seedlings can be planted. Is there room for one at school?

Look after birds. Put up a nesting-box (away from cats) and a bird table. Put out food and water in winter.

Make piles of logs or stones. Smaller creatures like to shelter in places like these.

Do you pass a hedge on your way to school? Look after it and keep it clear of litter.

Find some bare soil or waste ground nearby where you could sow some wildflower seeds.

Schools often have land around them. Is there room for a pond, tree or wildlife garden? Talk to a teacher about your ideas.

Join a local group that helps to protect the environment. Groups often need helpers to pick up litter, clear paths and so on.

Glossary

Compost The crumbly mixture we add to soil to help plants grow. Compost is made from rotted-down plants, fruit and vegetable peelings.

Concrete A hard grey material that is used for building. Concrete looks and feels like stone.

Endangered In danger of becoming extinct.

Environment The land, air and sea that make the world around us.

Extinct No longer living on Earth.

Fertilizer Something that is added to the soil to help plants grow.

Food chain A way of showing what eats what in a habitat. Some animals feed on plants and they are then eaten by other animals.

Fumes The mixture of dirt and gases that is made when cars burn fuel.

Gas A substance like air, which is not solid or liquid. Air is made of a mixture of different gases.

Habitat A place where wildlife lives.

Natural Something that has been made by nature and not by people.

Organic A way of growing food that uses only natural fertilizers and pest controls.

Oxygen A gas that is found in the air, and which all animals need to survive.

Pest An animal, often an insect, that feeds on and damages food crops.

Pollute To spoil the air, land or water with harmful substances.

Species A particular kind of animal or plant.

Index